Biddy Mason

The Open Hand

by Deborah Newton Chocolate

illustrated by Keaf Holliday

McGraw-Hill
School Division

New York   Farmington

It was a long, hard trip across the United States. Walking slowly in the dust behind a long wagon train was a black woman named Biddy Mason. It was her job to herd all her master's animals.

Biddy was a slave. She walked thousands of miles during the long trip from Mississippi to California.

Biddy didn't know it then, but that long trip would end in her freedom. It would also make her one of the richest black pioneers in all of California.

Biddy Mason was born in Georgia on August 15, 1818. Her name was Bridget, but everyone called her Biddy.

In time, Biddy was sold to Robert Smith of Mississippi. In 1848, Smith moved his family and slaves to Utah. In 1851, he continued the long trip west to California.

Life was hard for Biddy. She had to take care of all the animals. She also had to care for her own three children.

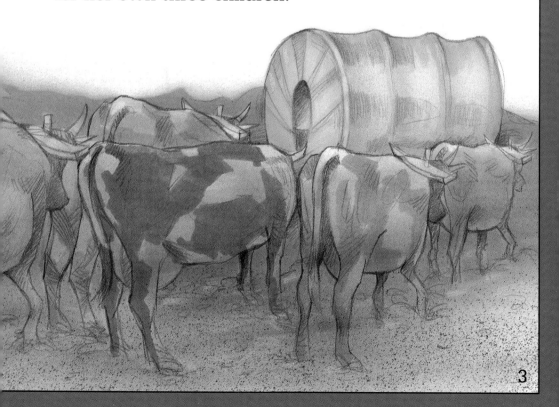

Smith settled in San Bernardino, California. There Biddy met some free blacks. They told her that California was a free state. Slavery was not allowed there.

Biddy's master was not happy to hear that California was free. He prepared to move to Texas, where slavery was allowed.

Meanwhile, Biddy's daughter, Ellen, fell in love with Charles Owens, a free black man. Charles did not want Biddy and Ellen to leave California. So he went to his father, Robert Owens, for help. Mr. Owens told the sheriff that Robert Smith was keeping slaves.

The sheriff went looking for Smith.

Robert Smith did not intend to give up his slaves without a fight. He and Biddy had to go to court. But California law did not allow blacks to testify against whites. Biddy was only allowed to speak with the judge alone.

The judge believed that Biddy wanted to stay in California. He granted freedom to her and all of her family.

Biddy was free for the first time in her
life. But she and her children could no
longer live with the Smith family. So, Robert
Owens kindly offered his home to Biddy and
her three children. Biddy and her family
moved in with the Owens family. Later,
Biddy's daughter, Ellen, married Charles
Owens.

Now that she had a place to live, Biddy set about finding work. When Biddy was a slave, she was a midwife and nurse to the women on the plantation. Now she found work delivering babies in Los Angeles County.

Biddy took other jobs, too. She worked with patients in the hospital and sick prisoners in jail.

Through all her hard work, Biddy had a dream. She wanted to save enough money to buy a home for herself and her children.

Ten long years passed. At last, Biddy had saved $250. That was enough to buy her own land.

Biddy became one of the first black women to own land in Los Angeles. She called part of her land "the Homestead." Biddy made her children promise never to sell that part of the land.

The land that Biddy bought was on the edge of town. Biddy built a few small wooden houses. Then she rented them out to earn money.

Now that she had land of her own, Biddy had another dream—to build some stores. Biddy wanted to make sure that her family would always be taken care of.

In 1884, Biddy Mason sold a small piece of her land for $1,500. She used the money to build a brick building with stores on the ground floor. She and her family lived on the second floor. Biddy rented out her ground-floor stores to shopkeepers. This earned her a great deal of money for her children and grandchildren.

By 1885, Biddy's two grandsons had grown up. She guided them and taught them the value of a dollar.

Biddy built a livery stable for them on part of her land. People could keep their horses there, and also rent horses to use.

Five years later, Biddy made her grandsons the owners of the stable. It was her way of showing how much she cared about her family.

Biddy Mason's love of family did not end with her own children and grandchildren. It included her neighbors—the poor people of Los Angeles County. Biddy used her money to help make Los Angeles County a good place to live and raise children.

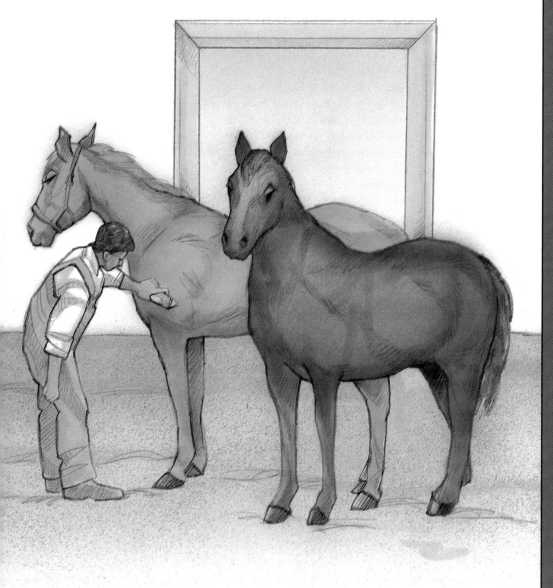

Biddy Mason and Charles Owens established the first black church in the city. It was the Los Angeles branch of the First African Methodist Episcopal Church. Biddy also paid for the land the church was on, as well as the minister's salary.

The poor always held a special place in Biddy's heart. She had a plan to help them. Biddy bought more land. Then she sold it for lots of money. Biddy used this money to buy food for families who needed help.

Word spread that Biddy Mason was a friend to those in need. Soon lines of people were waiting on her front step each morning.

In the years that followed, Biddy ran a nursery school in her home and started another school. Biddy strongly believed in the value of a good education. She did her best to give schooling to every child who needed it.

Biddy's oldest grandson, Robert Curry Owens, also bought and sold land. He and the rest of Biddy's family kept adding more land to the first piece that Biddy had bought.

Biddy Mason came to California a slave and ended up a free black woman. She bought her own land. She cared for those in need. And she helped Los Angeles County grow.

Biddy Mason died on January 15, 1891. In 1989, the city of Los Angeles called for a "Biddy Mason Day." A memorial was built on the land Biddy called "her Homestead."

Biddy's love was remembered in the words she told to her great-granddaughter, Gladys Owens Smith. As Biddy always said: "If you hold your hand closed, nothing good can come in. The open hand is blessed, for it gives in abundance, even as it receives."